by Tom Wilson

≣EXLEY

16 Chalk Hill, Watford, Herts, WD1 4BN

First published in Great Britain in 1984 by
Exley Publications Ltd, 16 Chalk Hill, Watford,
Herts WD1 4BN.

Printed and bound in Great Britain by Hazell Watson and
Viney Limited, member of BPCC Group, Aylesbury, Bucks.

ISBN 1 85015 018 4
ISBN 1 85015 021 4 (paperback)

Ziggy ™ is syndicated internationally by
Universal Press Syndicate.
Short People Arise! copyright © 1981 by
Universal Press Syndicate.

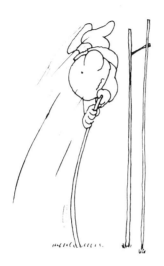

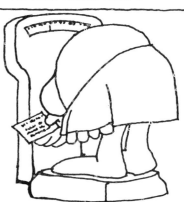

Dear Sirs,
to helps you in your fine work at the foundation, I would like to contribute my body to science
Sincerely yours,
ZIGGY
REJECTED
RETURN TO SENDER

ABRAMS
BOOKS
THE HOBBIT
Gnomes
..IT'S NICE TO SEE MY KIND OF PEOPLE FINALLY MAKING IT BIG !!

ELEVATOR
SHOES

UP PLEASE...

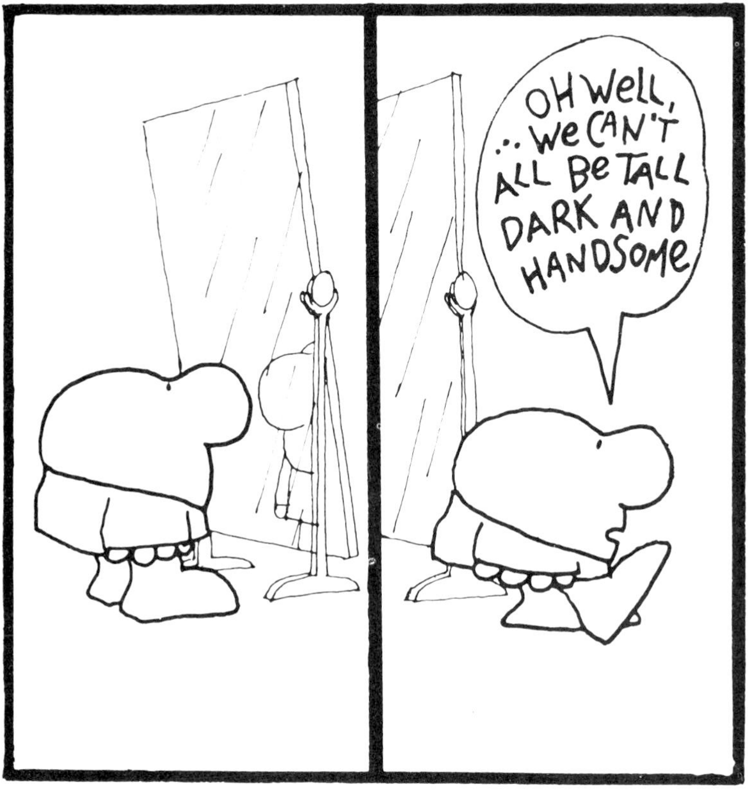
OH WELL, ... WE CAN'T ALL BE TALL DARK AND HANDSOME

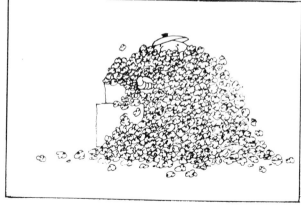

...IT'S TOO BIG FOR FIT, SIR, BUT IT'S JUST RIGHT FOR FUNKY !!
Tom Wilson

LISHEN SHORTY...
YOU AGREE WITH
ONE MORE THING
I SAY, AND I'M GONNA
SOCK YOU RIGHT ON
THE JAW!!

I'M SORRY, SIR, BUT SERGIO VALENTI DOESN'T WANT PEOPLE LIKE YOU WEARING HIS CLOTHES !!
Tom Wilson

YOUR COLLATERAL IS FINE... ...EVERYTHING SEEMS TO BE IN ORDER... NOW THERE IS OUR MINIMUM HEIGHT REQUIREMENT..
LOANS

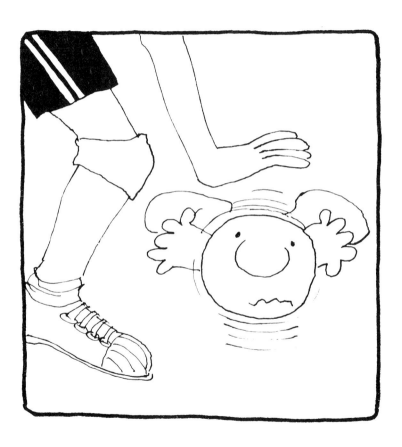

SORRY, MATE ... BUT i CALLS THEM THE WAY i SEES THEM.... ...AND YOU'RE NO CLINT EASTWOOD!
tom wilson

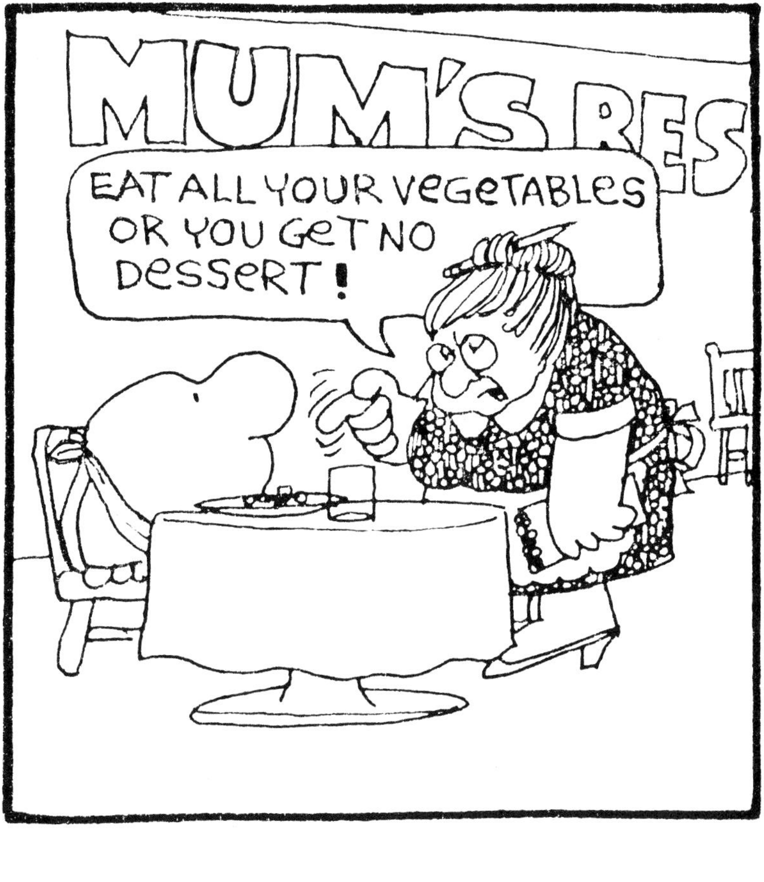
MUM'S RES
EAT ALL YOUR VEGETABLES OR YOU GET NO DESSERT!

...HELLO...THIS IS DIAL-A-JOKE... DID YOU HEAR THE ONE ABOUT THE SHORT, BALD-HEADED WALLY WITH THE BIG NOSE...?....

...i REALIZE THIS IS AN iDIOTIC QUESTION, BUT WOULD YOU MIND DATING A GIRL TALLER THAN YOU?
COMPUTER DATING
TOM WILSON

Other Ziggy books from Exley Publications

Ziggy: Plants are some of my favourite people, £2.95.
This an another popular book of Ziggy cartoons. Ziggy is a born
loser and his endearing failures make him appeal to all ages.
Ziggy and his plant have a very special relationship. His plant
reacts emotionally, complains a great deal, gets depressed a lot,
is jealous of the attention Ziggy gives any of his annuals and
hates being left alone. A must for anyone who is potty about
plants – or about Ziggy.
Ziggy: Pets are friends who share your rainy days, £2.95.
Ziggy's pets are very special little people who run his life
for him. Anyone who has loved a pet will see themselves in this
book.
Ziggy: Work is a lousy way to earn a living, £2.50.
A consolation book from Ziggy for all those mortals who trudge
to work in the morning. How Ziggy copes (or fails to!) with
inflation, his boss, the tax man and the rueful business of
making ends meet. An attractive, low cost little hardback.
Ziggy: Know how much I love you, £1.95.
This must be one of the smallest 'books' on sale: just
2¼ x 2¼ x 1 inch; yet the surpise concertina fold-out message
extends to nearly five feet in length. Packed in a pretty
heart-covered slip case this is a magic, zany little book that says
it all. Children, mums, dads, lovers, grandads – everyone would
love it on a special occasion.

Simply order through your bookshop, or by post from
Exley Publications Ltd, Dept ZIGO, 16 Chalk Hill,
Watford, Herts, WD1 4BN. Please add 60p as a contribution
to postage and packing.